Food Like Mine

My name is

....

My favorite food is

....

Alonso, age 9, Mexico

Hafsa, age 7, South Africa

DK

Senior Editor Carrie Love

Editor Sophia Danielsson-Waters

US Senior Editor Margaret Parrish

Senior Designers Lisa Robb, Elaine Hewson

Designers Rachael Hare, Pauline Marie Korp

Food Photographer Dave King

Home Economist and Recipe Writer Denise Smart

US Recipe Consultant Kate Ramos

Jacket Designer Lisa Robb

Jacket Coordinator Francesca Young

Pre-production Producer Nadine King

Producer Isabell Schart

Creative Technical Support Sonia Charbonnier

Managing Editor Penny Smith

Managing Art Editors Mabel Chan, Gemma Glover

Publisher Mary Ling

Creative Director Jane Bull

Consultants Michael Blake (Corn),
Annie Gray (Other staples), Stephen Harris (Wheat),
Renee Marton (Rice), and Andrew Smith (Potatoes)

First American Edition, 2017
Published in the United States by DK Publishing
345 Hudson Street, New York, New York 10014

Copyright © 2017 Dorling Kindersley Limited
DK, a Division of Penguin Random House LLC
17 18 19 20 21 10 9 8 7 6 5 4 3 2 1
001-285428-July/2017

Published in Great Britain by Dorling Kindersley Limited.

A catalog record for this book is available
from the Library of Congress.
ISBN: 978-1-4654-6135-3

DK books are available at special discounts when purchased in bulk
for sales promotions, premiums, fund-raising, or educational use.
For details, contact: DK Publishing Special
Markets, 345 Hudson Street, New York, New York 10014
SpecialSales@dk.com

Printed and bound in China

A WORLD OF IDEAS:
SEE ALL THERE IS TO KNOW

www.dk.com

⚠ Please note

All the recipes in this book are to be made under
adult supervision. When you see the warning triangle,
be extra careful, since a hot stove, electrical appliances,
and sharp implements are used in making a recipe.
Ask an adult to help you.

Kitchen rules

- When you're in the kitchen, you should ask an adult
to take pans in and out of the oven and to heat
things on the burner.
- Ask an adult to help if you need to use a sharp knife
or an electrical appliance.
- Wash your hands before and after you work with
food. Always wash your hands after handling raw
eggs and raw meat.
- Do not lick your fingers when you are working
with food.
- Check the use-by date on all ingredients.
- Follow the instructions on packaging that explain
how to store food.

Getting started

1. Read the recipe instructions all the way through before
you begin.
2. Gather everything you need.
3. Have a cloth handy to wipe up spills.
4. Put on an apron, tie back your hair, and wash
your hands.

Key to symbols

 How many people a dish **serves**, or how
many portions it **makes**.

 The time it takes to **prepare** a dish, including
chilling and marinating.

The time it takes to **cook** a dish.

CONTENTS

Jamie, age 8, New Zealand

Erel, age 7, Israel

The world of FOOD

Food is about more than just eating. It shows who we are, where we come from, and what we like. Eating habits are shaped by our culture and beliefs. Even what we eat for breakfast may seem strange to someone on the other side of the world. But one thing's certain—we're all united by food!

> More than one **TRILLION** chicken eggs are laid every year.

Ivan, age 7, Malaysia

Uncooked white **RICE** can last for up to **10** years.

Joaquin, age 11, USA

There are **1.5 BILLION** cows in the world.

CORN SYRUP can be found in **KETCHUP, SOFT DRINKS,** and **YOGURT.**

Clara, age 9, Germany

POTATOES
were the first food grown in **SPACE.**

The **spiciness** of chili peppers is measured on a scale called **SCOVILLES**.

Trini, age 10, Argentina

Joshua, age 8, Botswana

Types of FOOD

There are five main types of food. They help your body with different things and all foods have a job to do. Food gives you the energy to play, run, think, and grow. The biggest source of this energy comes from carbohydrates.

Portion advice varies, but a variety of different foods is healthy.

Jollof rice

Carbohydrates

Carbohydrates are starchy foods that usually come from grains (rice, wheat, corn, rye, barley, and oats). There are other sources too including vegetables and some fruits.

Bread

Select healthy whole-wheat varieties.

Carbohydrates help your muscle and organs to work well.

Brown rice

Couscous

Noodles

Oats

Rye

Corn

Breakfast cereal

Pasta dish

Yam

Sweet potato

Potato

Fruit and vegetables

This food group provides you with fiber, vitamins, and minerals. Fruit and vegetables help your body to heal itself, prevent infections, and keep your skin healthy.

Apple

Cabbage

Pumpkin

Mandarin orange

Tomato

Green beans

Protein

Protein is found in meat, but also in non-animal sources. Protein-rich foods help your body to repair and to grow.

Foods high in protein often contain vitamins and minerals, too.

Chicken

Egg

Lentils

Lamb is a great source of B vitamins.

Lamb

Fish

Peas

Beans

Soybeans

Nuts

Milk and dairy

This food group is high in calcium, which helps your nerves and muscles work well and strengthens your teeth and bones.

Fats help to maintain body heat and transport vitamins around your body.

Fats

It's best to choose foods containing healthy fats, such as the ones shown below.

Cheese is also rich in zinc and phosphorus.

Milk

Cheese

Yogurt

Olives

Oily fish

Avocado

What are STAPLE foods?

Staple foods are the filling foods people eat regularly around the world—sometimes as part of every meal. They give us a large amount of calories, and are generally easy to grow and store. Even better, they're usually cheap to buy, accessible all year round, and won't spoil quickly. With all these positives, it's no wonder we eat them so much!

The **four** main staples are all edible plants. There are about **200,000** edible plants in the world, but only **0.1%** are regularly eaten by people.

1

Rice is eaten regularly by more than half the people in the world.

RICE

WHEAT

2

Wheat is used to make bread, which is eaten almost everywhere.

3

Corn is especially important in the Americas.

CORN

POTATOES

Potatoes are eaten by more than a billion people worldwide.

4

Other staples are **legumes**, certain **fruits**, **meat**, **fish**, **dairy**, and some **root vegetables**.

RICE

This tiny grain is eaten in every country in the world. It is an integral part of our diet and provides us with lots of energy. In many countries, rice is eaten at every mealtime and as a snack. It's a key part of our past and an even more important part of our future.

The continent that grows the **MOST** rice is **ASIA.**

Rice is eaten **TWICE** a day by **two-thirds** of the world's population.

When rice is cooked it swells to **3 times** its original **WEIGHT.**

There are more than ~~00~~ ...own

Rice was used to strengthen the Great **WALL** of China.

Rice is used in lots of **COSMETICS.**

FIELDS OF RICE

Rice needs a lot of water to grow. Farmers often flood the land they want to grow rice on, or use land that is already flooded to ensure a good crop. These flooded areas are called "paddy fields."

Ducks and fish often live in paddy fields. They eat pests and weeds that would otherwise harm the rice plants.

RICE is important for the FUTURE because it can withstand a slight rise in global temperature, whereas WHEAT and CORN will struggle more.

Growing RICE

Rice is primarily grown in paddy fields and terraces around the world. It usually takes 3–4 months to grow, from planting the s to harvesting the grains. R milled before it's cooked

Growing rice

The soil in a field or terrace is **plowed** and **tilled** (dug up and mixed together), then leveled back out. Then rice seedlings are planted by hand or machine. Once the rice is fully grown, it's gathered by hand or by a combine harvester.

Seedling

Harvesting by hand

Nearly 95% of all RICE is EATEN in the country where it is grown.

Rice plant

Harvesting by machine

The part of rice that we eat is called the grain (also called the seed)

Hull

Bran

From paddy to plate

Before rice can be eaten, it must be dried out and go through a milling process. The grain is separated from the hull (hard outer casing) as well as the bran layer. However, if brown rice is desired, the bran layer is left on the grain. Otherwise, you get white rice.

13

Types of rice

There are more than 40,000 varieties of rice, but they all fall into two main categories—Asian rice and African rice. All rice is described by the length of its grain once it's been cooked (short, medium, or long).

Rice comes in lots of colors: white, brown, purple, red, and black.

Uses for rice

Rice is often ground into flour and used to make a variety of foods such as noodles, paper rolls, and cakes. Rice can also be puffed and made into cereal and crackers.

Rice flour

Fresh rice noodles

DELICIOUS DOSAS

These folded crepes are made from rice flour and lentils. They are eaten as a snack or as a meal.

Dosa

Dried rice noodles

Another common way of describing rice is by whether it's "sticky" or "less-sticky" once it's cooked.

Rice is heated in a circular mold and puffs up to fill the space. ……>

Rice paper rolls

Puffed rice cereal

These rice cakes are eaten at Chinese New Year. ……>

Rice cake

Sweet rice cakes

Short-grain

Also called "round-grain rice," short-grain rice is up to ¼in (5mm) long. This type always sticks together when it's cooked.

Short-grain rice is used to make sushi, sweet rice dishes, porridge, and dumplings.

Like Asian rice, African rice has short-, medium-, and long-grain varieties.

Camargue red rice

Arborio rice

American short-grain rice

Medium-grain

Medium-grain rice is ⅛–¼in (5mm–6mm) long. The grains are tender and moist and usually cling together when cooked.

Medium-grain rice may be used for paellas and creamy rice desserts.

This type contains lots of iron.

Brown standard rice

Spanish bomba rice

Chinese black rice

Long-grain

Any rice that is ¼in (6mm) or longer is called long-grain. This rice can be white or brown and is light and fluffy when cooked.

Long-grain rice is ideal for making side dishes, soups, pilafs, salads, and stuffings.

Jasmine rice

Basmati rice has a nutlike flavor.

Basmati rice

Red cargo

American long-grain rice

Whether it's in a main meal or used in sweet treats or snacks, rice is always a staple you can rely on. There are rice dishes for every time of day, from breakfast to lunch and dinner.

Daifuku, Japan

This Japanese sweet treat is made from mochi—a sticky rice cake that is pounded into a paste. It has a sweet bean filling, called anko.

RICE around

Kedgeree, UK

This spiced rice and lentil dish is often eaten for breakfast and usually contains smoked fish, such as haddock.

Khalifa, age 6, Bahrain

Qoozi, Bahrain

Qoozi is popular in Bahrain and the countries nearby. It's a dish of lamb, nuts, currants, and vegetables, all served on a bed of rice.

Songpyeon, South Korea

These rice cakes are stuffed with either a sweet or savory filling. They are commonly eaten at a Korean harvest festival celebration.

Yeh-Lin, age 9, South Korea

Arancini, Italy

Crunchy outside and soft inside, arancini are breaded rice balls that are deep fried. They are usually eaten as an appetizer or a snack.

the world

Cooked white rice

Naiyarat (Knight), age 8, Thailand

Pad Thai, Thailand

A popular street food in Thailand, pad thai is a mixture of rice noodles, firm tofu, vegetables, and often seafood.

Lucas, age 6, Spain

Biryani, India

Basmati rice is the main ingredient of this savory meal. Biryani can contain meat, fish, or vegetables and is spiced differently from region to region.

Paella, Spain

This dish mixes rice with seafood, vegetables, or chicken and sausage. It's cooked in a large, shallow pan and comes from Valencia in Spain.

Congee, China

This is a creamy rice porridge dish. It's a comfort food and is popular all over the world—especially in Asia.

Vegetable sushi rolls

These rice rolls are filled with vegetables and wrapped in seaweed. They are served with pickled ginger, wasabi paste, and soy sauce.

YOU WILL NEED:

- *bamboo mat*
- 1 cup sushi rice
- 1¼ cups water
- 2 tbsp white wine vinegar
- 1 tbsp sugar
- ½ tsp salt
- ¼ cucumber
- ½ small carrot
- ½ small red bell pepper
- ½ small yellow bell pepper
- 4 nori (seaweed) sheets

TO SERVE:

- pickled ginger
- soy sauce
- wasabi paste (optional)

1

Rinse the rice with cold water until the water runs clear. Put the rice in a pan. Add the water.

2

Bring the rice to a boil. Reduce the heat and cover. Simmer for 10 minutes. Remove from the heat and leave to steam.

3

Meanwhile, warm the vinegar, sugar, and salt in a small pan until they dissolve.

4

Spread the rice onto a baking sheet. Pour the vinegar mixture evenly over the rice and mix gently. Let cool.

5

Remove the seeds from the cucumber with a spoon. Cut the cucumber, carrots, and peppers into equal strips—24 in total.

6

Shiny side down

Put 1 sheet of nori on a bamboo mat. With wet hands, spread ¼ of the rice over the nori. Add 6 vegetable strips, as shown.

7

Using the bamboo mat, roll the sushi up tightly. The nori will seal to itself naturally when you reach the end.

8

Using a wet knife, trim the edges and cut into 6 slices. Repeat steps 6–8 to make the rest of the sushi rolls.

Sushi rolls are a popular dish globally, but they originated in Japan, where Sotaro is from.

Jollof rice

This one-pot rice dish is colored an orangey red by the juice from the tomatoes. It is popular in many West African countries.

YOU WILL NEED:
- 2 tbsp sunflower oil
- 1 large onion, chopped
- 1 clove garlic, crushed
- 14oz (400g) can chopped tomatoes
- 1 red bell pepper, seeded and chopped
- 2 tbsp tomato paste
- salt and freshly ground black pepper
- 1 tsp chili powder
- 1 tsp curry powder
- 1 bay leaf
- sprig fresh thyme
- 2½ cups chicken or vegetable stock
- 1 cup basmati or long-grain rice, rinsed under cold water
- 4 skinless, boneless chicken breasts

1 Heat 1 tablespoon of the oil in a pan. Cook the onions and garlic over low heat for 4–5 minutes, until soft.

2 Stir in the chopped tomatoes, red bell pepper, and tomato paste, then season with salt and freshly ground black pepper.

3 Add the chili powder, curry powder, bay leaf, and thyme, then pour in the stock.

4 Bring to a boil, then reduce the heat. Cover and simmer for 5 minutes.

5 Add the rice. Bring to a boil. Reduce the heat to low. Cover and simmer for 25 minutes, or until most of the liquid is absorbed.

6 Brush the chicken with the remaining oil. Grill for 5–6 minutes on each side, until cooked through and golden.

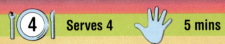

TOP TIP
Serve with chicken or fish. For a vegetarian option, add a side of vegetables instead.

Jedidiah is from Ghana, where jollof rice is a traditional meal. It's often served with fried plantain.

Indian rice pudding

TOP TIP
Replace the pistachios with cashews or almonds if you prefer.

In India, this dish is called "kheer" in the north and "payasam" in the south. There are many regional variations for this recipe, which can be eaten during a meal or as a dessert.

YOU WILL NEED:

- ½ cup basmati rice
- 3¼ cups whole milk
- 3 tbsp sugar
- ½ tsp ground cardamom
- ½ tsp grated nutmeg
- ⅓ cup golden raisins or raisins
- ⅓ cup pistachios, chopped

1

Put the rice, milk, and sugar in a saucepan and bring to a boil. Reduce the heat and simmer for 10 minutes.

2

Stir in the cardamom, nutmeg, and golden raisins. Reserve a few pistachios for decoration and stir in the rest.

3

Continue to cook over low heat for another 10 minutes, stirring often, until the mixture is thick and creamy.

4

Spoon the rice into 4 serving dishes. Serve warm or cover and chill in the fridge to serve cold later.

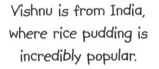

Vishnu is from India, where rice pudding is incredibly popular.

5

Before serving, decorate with the reserved pistachios.

WHEAT

This bristly grass is one of the most important edible plants in the world. It's a staple food for billions of people and is grown almost everywhere. Wheat grains are ground into flour and used to make all kinds of food—from cakes and pastries to bread and pasta.

Wheat is a staple food for more than **35%** of the world's population.

Grains of wheat have been found in ancient Egyptian **TOMBS**.

Wheat takes up more **LAND** than **any** other crop.

Today, it takes less than **10 SECONDS** to harvest enough wheat for **70 BREAD LOAVES.**

Wheat and barley were the first grain crops to **EVER** be farmed.

Each person in Italy eats more than **50**lb **(23**kg**)** of pasta per year.

HUGE HARVEST

People used to cut down wheat crops using sharp knives. Now, people use combine harvesters to harvest wheat. A combine can chop down 1 acre (0.4 hectares) of wheat in 6 minutes. That would take a person half a day!

Wheat crops are ready to harvest when they turn bright yellow.

China produces and eats the most wheat.

Growing WHEAT

Wheat is easy to grow and can be found all over the world—in high and low areas, and in hot and cold places. No matter what month it is, wheat is being harvested somewhere in the world.

Mighty machine

A combine harvester does many tasks at once. It **reaps** (cuts down the wheat crop), **threshes** (separates stalks from spikelets), and **winnows** (separates grains from chaff). It also **stores** grains in a tank.

Wheat plant

The spike (head) of the plant is made up of little spikelets.

A spikelet contains wheat grains, which are encased in chaff.

Stalk

Chaff

Leaf

Grain

Each spike of wheat has 40–60 grains!

ADAPTABLE GRASS

Today's wheat gives more grains and is more resistant to disease than ever before. Wheat stalks are also shorter than 100 years ago because it's easier to harvest short, upright plants that don't bend over.

What's next?

The wheat grains are taken to a factory, where they're poured into machines, ready for processing. Most grains are then milled (ground down) into flour.

Types of wheat

When it's growing in the fields, wheat looks like bristly grass. By the time it's milled into flour or semolina, however, it looks completely different.

Early wheat

Wild varieties, such as "einkorn" and "emmer" grew more than 9,000 years ago. Over time, people grew wheat with more grains that clung to the stalks, making them easier to harvest.

Einkorn

Emmer

People used to grind wheat by rolling a big stone over a flat stone. Hard work!

Common wheat

This is the most widely grown wheat species today. More than 90 percent of all wheat is common wheat.

Common wheat grains

Common wheat

You can also eat wheat grains raw.

Durum wheat

Durum wheat is a special type of wheat that is very hard. This means it keeps its shape when it's cooked.

Durum grains

Durum wheat

Wheat to semolina

Durum wheat is ground into coarse semolina, which is used to make couscous, grits, and pasta.

Semolina is mixed with water (or eggs) to make a dough. It's rolled out, cut into pasta shapes, and then left to dry.

Semolina

Pasta shapes

Common wheat is too soft to make into pasta—the shapes would fall apart when cooked.

Wheat to flour

Wheat grains are often milled into flour. There are many types of flour, which differ depending on which part of the wheat grain is used.

White flour is made from only part of the wheat grain.

Whole-wheat flour is made from all of the wheat grain.

White self-rising flour

Light brown whole-wheat flour

All-purpose white flour

Flour power!

Bread is made by combining flour with other ingredients, including water and yeast. There are all sorts of bread recipes around the world.

Bread can also be made from rice, corn, and potato flour.

A common Indian bread.

Roti

Baguettes

Sliced, brown bread

Popular in the Middle East.

Pita

Doughnuts, USA

Doughnuts are deep-fried pastries. They are popular worldwide, but more than 10 BILLION are eaten every year in the US!

Isn't it amazing that all these different dishes were made from the same basic ingredient? Wheat is so versatile, it's used in staple meals, snacks, and sweet treats.

Solal, age 7, France

Wonderful

Quiche Lorraine, France

Quiches are deep pies. The outer pastry is made from wheat and then it's filled with a savory egg custard and yummy extras, such as bacon.

Bassma, age 8, Morocco

Couscous, Morocco

It may look like fluffy rice, but couscous is made from balls of semolina— a flour made from durum wheat. Couscous dishes often include meat, spices, and vegetables.

Noodle soup, China

Noodles are usually made from rice or wheat. Wheat noodles are used in this Chinese soup, which is popular all over Asia.

WHEAT

Whole-wheat bread roll

Lasagne, Italy

Durum wheat is used to make pasta, including flat lasagne sheets. The sheets are layered between sauces and fillings, and then everything is baked in an oven.

Martyna, age 10, Poland

Apple cake, Poland

Traditional Polish apple cakes are made from a sweet pastry and have a spiced apple filling.

Khurrshuur, Mongolia

Dumplings wrap up other foods. For khurrshuur, the inside surprise is usually meat or potatoes.

Robert, age 9, Mongolia

Clara and Lucy, age 9, Australia

Anzac cookies, Australia

Named after the Australian and New Zealand Army Corps (ANZAC), these cookies were once hard and savory, but now are sweet and often flavored with coconut.

Four ways with pasta

Durum wheat is used to make more than 350 types of pasta. Follow the instructions to make a basic pasta, then choose from four of these delicious sauce recipes.

Bring lightly salted water to a boil in a large saucepan. Add the dried pasta and cook for 10–12 minutes.

Drain the pasta in a colander, then stir the pasta into the sauce.

TOP TIP
Use 1 cup of dried pasta per person.

Bolognese sauce

- 1 tbsp olive oil
- 1 onion, chopped
- 1 clove garlic, crushed
- 1 carrot, diced
- 1lb (450g) ground beef
- ¾ cup beef stock
- 14oz (400g) can chopped tomatoes
- 2 tbsp tomato paste
- 2 tsp dried mixed herbs

1. Heat the oil in a pan and add the onion, garlic, and carrot. Cook over medium heat for 4–5 minutes, until softened. **2.** Add the beef and cook until browned. Stir in the stock, tomatoes, tomato paste, and herbs. Bring to a boil. **3.** Reduce the heat, cover, and simmer for 15 minutes, until thickened.

Vegetable pasta sauce

- 1 small red onion, cut into 8 wedges
- 1 red bell pepper and 1 yellow bell pepper, seeded and chopped
- 1 zucchini, chopped
- 1 clove garlic, crushed
- 2 tbsp olive oil
- ¾ cup tomato paste (or chopped tomatoes)
- handful fresh basil, torn
- salt

1. Mix the vegetables, garlic, and olive oil in a bowl. **2.** Heat a large grill pan. Add the vegetables and cook for 3 minutes, turning occasionally, until lightly charred. **3.** Place in a large saucepan. Stir in the tomato paste and bring to a boil. Simmer for 5 minutes. Stir in the basil and season to taste.

Four cheese sauce

- 2 tbsp softened butter
- 2 tbsp all-purpose flour
- ½ cup milk
- 2½oz (75g) grated aged Cheddar cheese
- ¼ cup finely grated Parmesan cheese
- 2½oz (75g) soft cream cheese
- 2½oz (75g) mild blue cheese, crumbled
- salt and freshly ground black pepper

1. Place the butter, flour, and milk in a pan. Cook over medium heat, whisking nonstop, until the mixture is smooth and thick. **2.** Remove from the heat and stir in the cheeses. Place over low heat and cook, stirring nonstop until the cheese melts. Season to taste.

Pesto sauce

- ⅓ cup pine nuts
- 2 cloves garlic, chopped
- 1 tsp sea salt
- 1¾oz (50g) fresh basil leaves
- 1¼ cups fresh Parmesan cheese, grated
- ¾ cup extra virgin olive oil

1. Place the pine nuts in a frying pan. Lightly toast for 2–3 minutes over medium heat. **2.** Puree the nuts, garlic, salt, and basil leaves in a food processor. Transfer to a bowl, then stir in the cheese. Slowly beat in the oil. **3.** To store, place the pesto in a storage jar and cover with olive oil. Keep in the fridge for up to a week.

Vegetable chow mein

This Chinese meal shows off classic Asian flavors, such as ginger, soy sauce, and sesame oil. Serve this dish as a vegetarian main course or add meat or fish to boost the level of protein.

YOU WILL NEED:

- 3 cups dried medium egg noodles
- 1 tbsp sunflower oil
- 1 clove garlic, crushed
- 1 tsp freshly grated fresh ginger
- 4 scallions, sliced
- 2 carrots, peeled and cut into thin strips
- 4½oz (125g) shitake mushrooms, sliced
- 3½oz (100g) snow peas
- 2 tbsp light soy sauce
- 2 tbsp oyster sauce
- ½ tsp toasted sesame oil
- 3½oz (100g) bean sprouts

This tasty meal is from China, where Shaowei lives. It's also a popular dish around the world.

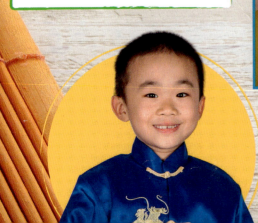

1

Place the noodles in a pan of boiling water and simmer for 4 minutes.

2

Drain well, then return the noodles to the pan to keep them warm.

3

Heat the sunflower oil in a wok and add the garlic, ginger, and scallions. Stir-fry for 2–3 minutes.

4

Add the carrots, mushrooms, and snow peas. Cook for an additional 2–3 minutes.

5

In a bowl, mix together the soy sauce, oyster sauce, and sesame oil.

6

Add the bean sprouts, noodles, and sauce. Make sure everything is coated with the sauce. Cook for 2–3 minutes.

Four ways with pizza

It's really easy to make your own pizza. Just follow the recipe for pizza dough, cover with sauce, and add your chosen toppings.

YOU WILL NEED:

- 2 cups white bread flour, plus extra for dusting
- ½ tsp salt
- ½ tsp fast-acting dried yeast
- ¾ cup warm water
- 1 tbsp extra-virgin olive oil

1 Put the flour, salt, and yeast in a large mixing bowl. Make a well in the center. Stir in the water and oil to form a dough.

2 Place the dough on a lightly floured surface and knead for 7–10 minutes, until smooth and stretchy.

3 Place the dough in a lightly oiled bowl. Cover with plastic wrap. Leave to rise in a warm place for 1 hour, or until doubled in size.

4 Preheat the oven to 425°F (220°C). Lightly oil a pizza pan.

5 Punch the dough to knock out air bubbles. Knead on a floured surface. Roll the dough out into a 12in (30cm) circle.

6 Put the dough on the pizza pan, then add sauce and toppings. See right for topping ideas and baking times.

Alsatian tarte flambée

- 7oz (200g) ricotta cheese, fromage blanc, or Greek yogurt
- ½ cup crème fraîche
- ½ tsp ground nutmeg
- 4½oz (125g) smoked bacon, thinly sliced
- 1 onion, thinly sliced

Mix the ricotta with the crème fraîche and nutmeg. Spread over the pizza, then top with the bacon and onion. Cook for 10–12 minutes.

Margherita

- 6 tbsp pizza sauce
- 1oz (25g) grated mozzarella cheese
- 9oz (250g) pack mozzarella, drained and sliced
- 2 tomatoes, sliced
- fresh basil leaves

Spread the sauce over the pizza. Sprinkle the grated cheese over the top. Add the sliced mozzarella and tomatoes. Cook for 10–15 minutes. Garnish with the basil leaves.

Florentine

- 6 tbsp pizza sauce
- 1¾oz (50g) grated mozzarella cheese
- 8oz (225g) spinach leaves, cooked
- 1¾oz (50g) mozzarella ball, torn
- 4 eggs

Spread the sauce over the pizza. Add the grated cheese, spinach, and the torn mozzarella. Cook for 8 minutes. Crack the eggs on top. Cook for 3–4 minutes more.

Hawaiian

- 6 tbsp pizza sauce
- 3oz (85g) grated mozzarella cheese
- 1¾oz (50g) mozzarella ball, torn
- 1¾oz (50g) ham, chopped
- 3 pineapple rings, from a can, chopped

Spread the sauce over the pizza, then add the cheese, ham, and pineapple. Cook for 10–12 minutes.

Gingerbread cookies

Gingerbread tastes great and makes the house smell wonderful as it bakes. This recipe can be used for cookies, pretty decorations, or gingerbread people.

TOP TIP
Let the gingerbread cookies cool on the baking sheets before removing them.

YOU WILL NEED:

- 2 large baking sheets, lined with parchment paper
- 9 tbsp unsalted butter, diced
- ½ cup dark brown sugar
- ¼ cup molasses
- 1 tsp baking soda
- 2½ cups all-purpose flour, plus extra for dusting
- 2 tsp ground ginger
- ½ tsp ground cloves
- ½ tsp ground nutmeg
- ½ tsp ground cinammon

FOR THE ICING:

- 2 cups confectioners' sugar
- 2 tbsp water

TO DECORATE:

- Sugar sprinkles

Clara is 9 years old and lives in Germany, where gingerbread is sold at festive winter markets.

1

Melt the butter, sugar, and molasses in a pan over low heat until the butter and sugar have dissolved. Set aside to cool.

2

Sift the baking soda, flour, and spices into a large bowl and stir together.

3

Pour in the molasses and use a wooden spoon to mix well, until you have a soft, slightly sticky dough.

4

Wrap the dough in plastic wrap and chill in the refrigerator for 30 minutes. Preheat the oven to 350°F (180°C).

5

Roll out the dough on a floured surface until it's ¼in (5mm) thick. Cut out shapes; put on baking sheets. Bake for 9 minutes.

6

Decorate the cookies.

Sift the confectioners' sugar into a bowl. Add the water a little at a time, until the icing spreads easily.

CORN

Millions of people rely on corn for the main part of their diet. Corn is often cooked and eaten on the cob, but it can also be popped, boiled, roasted, ground into flour, or grilled. People use corn to feed livestock and even to provide fuel for transportation.

CHICKENS that eat a lot of corn have slightly **YELLOW** skin.

Corn is one of the ingredients used to make **chewing gum.**

On average, a corncob has **800** kernels in **16 ROWS.**

Corn is used to sweeten **SOFT DRINKS.**

HUSKS from corn are used by Native Americans to make mats and baskets.

The United States grows the most corn in the world.

Corn can grow up to 12ft (3.5m) high.

Growing CORN

Corn is one of the most useful and versatile crops in the world. It's a domesticated grass, which means it doesn't grow in the wild. Corn is grown on every continent except Antarctica.

Corn plants

Corn is grown in fields in large quantities. Seeds are planted in moist and rich soil. It takes between 2–3 months from planting the seeds to harvesting. Corn needs warm weather to grow. It's sensitive to frost, so if it's planted too early an entire crop can be lost.

Corn plant

Silks

Kernels are attached to a central cob.

Husk

Kernels

Cobs always have an even number of rows of kernels.

Until the 1930s, corn was mostly harvested by hand.

Harvesttime

If corn is being eaten as a vegetable it's picked when the silks are green. However, if it's grown as a grain, it's picked when the silks are brown. Corn is usually harvested by a machine called a mechanical corn picker.

Types of corn

Corn comes in many colors and sizes. If it's picked early, corn is eaten as a vegetable, but if corn is picked when it's fully grown, it's used as a grain.

Flint corn

The outer layer of the kernel for this type of corn is strong and hard. The kernels are often dried and ground into flour or polenta.

Flint corn

The white end of a kernel is called a "tip cap."

Polenta

Kernels

Corn flakes are toasted kernels.

Corn flakes

Cornmeal

Popcorn has more iron (an essential mineral) than roast beef or spinach.

Popcorn kernels are usually cooked in oil.

POPCORN

Popcorn is a type of flint corn. When the kernels are heated, the water inside of them turns into steam. The pressure created by the steam makes the kernels pop!

Baby corn is corn that's harvested early.

Baby corn is eaten raw or cooked. It's picked from the plant before the stalks are fully grown.

STREET FOOD

Corn was first grown 9,000 years ago, in what is modern-day Mexico. It's still popular there today, especially when it's heated and eaten on the cob.

Baby corn

Flour corn

Flour corn is usually used in baked food items. It comes in lots of colors, including yellow, red, blue, black, and multicolor.

These are made from a blue variety of flour corn.

Flour corn

Corn chips

Flour corn

Corn flour

These tacos are made from corn flour.

Corn chips

Tacos

Pod corn is an unusual variety because each kernel is encased in its own husk!

Dent corn

Dent corn is also called "field corn." Dents form as the kernels dry. It's used for animal feed, to make plastic, and to create fuel.

Dents

Dent corn

Sweet corn

Sweet corn is grown to be eaten as a vegetable. It's harvested early, when the kernels are soft and tender.

Sweet corn is usually canned or frozen to keep it fresh.

Canned sweet corn

One of the best things about corn, which in some countries is called maize, is that it can be used to make lots of delicious meals. Many countries have a famous dish that uses corn as the main ingredient.

Yohanna, age 7, Ethiopia

Popcorn, Ethiopia

Popcorn is traditionally served as part of an Ethiopian coffee ceremony. The coffee is prepared carefully—it's brewed three times.

Amazing

Tamales, Mexico

This Mexican street food contains a sweet or savory filling wrapped in a "masa" dough and then steamed in a corn husk. The husk is discarded before eating.

Andrea, age 7, South Carolina, USA

Grits, USA

Dried corn kernels are ground down to make grits. This porridge-like dish is often served as part of a meal. It can have shrimp, bacon, cheese, or butter on top.

Corn fritters, Thailand

A batter is made from flour, corn, egg, scallions, and coriander. The batter is fried in oil until golden. and served with a sweet chili dip.

CORN

Cymian, age 10, Montana, USA

Corn on the cob, USA

This is a popular side dish worldwide. It's often served with melted butter on top. Historically, Native Americans ate corn that was boiled or roasted.

Corn Kernels

Corn chowder, Jamaica

Creamy and tasty, this soup is made from a base of coconut milk. The chilis and cayenne pepper give it a spicy kick.

Grilled polenta, Italy

To make polenta, corn is ground into a flour and mixed with oil, salt, and water in a saucepan. It's then poured into a dish and grilled in the oven.

Ugali, Tanzania

Ugali is made from cornmeal and is cooked in boiling liquid. It has the consistency of oatmeal and is a staple dish in parts of Africa.

Shigo, age 7, Tanzania

Chicken fajitas

Serve this lightly spiced chicken and vegetable dish on corn tortillas, which are thin, unleavened flat breads made from finely ground corn.

Alonso is from Mexico. "Tex-mex" cuisine (such as fajitas) is a fusion of Texan and Mexican food.

YOU WILL NEED:

- 1lb (450g) skinless, boneless chicken breasts, cut into thin strips
- 1 red bell pepper, seeded and sliced
- 1 yellow bell pepper, seeded and sliced
- 1 red onion, sliced
- 1 tsp smoked paprika
- 1 tsp ground cumin
- 1 tsp mild chili powder
- 1 tsp dried oregano
- 1 lime
- 1 tbsp sunflower oil
- ½ tsp freshly ground black pepper

TO SERVE:

- 8 corn tortillas
- tomato salsa
- sour cream
- guacamole

1 Place the chicken, bell peppers, and onion in a large bowl, then add all the spices.

2 Finely grate the zest from the lime rind. Use a handheld juicer to squeeze all the juice from the lime.

3 Add the lime zest and juice, the seasoning, and 1 teaspoon of the oil. Stir well to coat the chicken and vegetables.

4 Heat the remaining oil in a frying pan. Add the chicken mixture and cook for 6–8 minutes, until cooked through.

5 Warm the corn tortillas according to the instructions on the package. Add the chicken, salsa, sour cream, and guacamole.

6 Fold the tortilla over or roll it up. Serve immediately.

Cornbread

This recipe is really simple to make. The scallions give it an interesting texture and taste. Cornbread is best served warm. It is perfect as a healthy snack or as a side dish.

YOU WILL NEED:

- 8in (20cm) square cake pan
- Butter to grease pan
- 1 tbsp baking powder
- 1⅓ cups coarse cornmeal (polenta)
- 5 scallions, finely chopped
- 1 tsp salt
- 2 large eggs
- 1¼ cups buttermilk, or milk or plain yogurt with a squeeze of lemon juice
- 4 tbsp butter, melted and cooled

1

Butter the square cake pan. Line the bottom with parchment paper. Preheat the oven to 400°F (200°C).

2

Place the baking powder, cornmeal, scallions, and salt in a large bowl. Combine well with a wooden spoon.

3

Put the eggs, buttermilk, and melted butter in a measuring cup and mix together.

4

Pour the egg mixture into the dry ingredients and stir well to combine the ingredients.

5

Pour the mixture in the pan and then use a spatula to smooth the top. Bake for 25–30 minutes, until golden.

6

Let the cornbread cool in the pan for 10 minutes, then turn it onto a cutting board. Remove the paper. Cut into 24 squares.

TOP TIP
Any remaining cornbread can be stored in the fridge for up to 2 days.

Cornbread is popular in the United States, where Lily is from. She lives in Ohio.

POTATOES

More than one billion people regularly eat potatoes. Potatoes were once grown only in the mountains of South America, but are now the most widely grown, non-grass crop in the world. Throughout history, potatoes have been a huge part of people's diets because they are so versatile and full of filling carbohydrates.

More than **420 MILLION** tons (380 million metric tons) of potatoes are grown each year.

POTATOES and **TOMATOES** come from the same plant family.

Pictures of potatoes can be seen on ancient South American **POTTERY.**

The average potato is made up of **80%** water.

Too much light makes potatoes turn **GREEN.**

The Inca people who lived long ago measured **TIME** by how long it took to cook a potato.

POTATO PLANTING

On a farm, a farmer plows the land, removing any stones that may get in the potatoes' way. Seed potatoes are then planted far apart in rows using a potato planting machine.

Potato production has grown in ASIA and AFRICA because of INVESTMENT, RESEARCH, and new growing TECHNOLOGIES.

Growing POTATOES

Potatoes are easy to grow, transport, and sell. In the past 50 years, production has increased more than any other crop, especially in Asia and Africa.

A sprouting seed potato

Shoots sprout from a potato's "eyes".

SEED START

Potatoes are grown from other potatoes, called "seed potatoes." Seed potatoes ensure that all potatoes grown will be exactly the same type.

Potato plant

Leaves

Stem

Seed potato

Developing tuber

Roots

Full-grown potato

Potatoes grow in both high and low, and hot and cold places.

Growing underground

The potatoes we eat are the underground "tubers" of the potato plant. Tubers are the enlarged parts of the plant's stem. They grow under the soil, and get all their nutrients from the plant above.

DEADLY DISEASE

Blight is a disease that destroys potato crops. It caused crop failure all over Europe in the 1800s.

Ready to pick

Potatoes are ready to be dug up when the plant leaves start to wither. A harvester lifts potatoes out from the soil. Dirt and soil are removed before the potatoes are taken to a factory.

Potatoes are...

☑ full of minerals (when the skin's left on)

☑ a good source of Vitamin C

Types of potato

There are more than 4,500 types of potatoes. They vary in color, and can look like teeny tiny balls, big bulky rocks, or even knobby fingers!

Potatoes are used to make chips, a popular snack worldwide.

The most nutritious part of a potato is just inside the skin.

Waxy

Some potatoes have waxy skins. This means their skin stays on when cooked, so they're best when boiled and steamed.

These potatoes can only be grown in Jersey, a small island between England and France.

Jersey Royal (International Kidney)

Charlotte

knobby potatoes like this are called "fingerlings"

Bintje

The most widely grown potato of France and Belgium.

Anya

Pink fir apple

Red La Soda

Marfona

Small ("new") potatoes are usually waxy, and are dug up before any other potatoes.

FREEZE-DRIED

In South America, potatoes are laid out in fields. There they are frozen at night and are bleached by the sun in the day. People also stomp on them with bare feet to get rid of excess liquid. This creates a long-lasting product called chuño.

Potatoes high in starch are ideal for making fluffy mashed potatoes.

Starchy

Other potatoes have floury, starchy skins. This means their skin falls off when cooked. They're better baked, roasted, and mashed.

Some potatoes are purple!

Vitelotte

Arran Victory

King Edward

Russet

Starchy potatoes make great potato chips and fries.

Maris Piper

Fries

All-purpose

These potatoes have a medium amount of starch—they fall in between starchy and waxy potatoes.

Purple Majesty

Yukon Gold

Rooster

You can use all-purpose potatoes to make baked potatoes.

Desirée

Accent

Boil them, fry them, mash them… there are so many things you can do with potatoes. They're great to accompany a main meal and are equally delicious when they take center stage.

Rösti, Switzerland

Swiss-German farmers originally ate rösti for breakfast, but now it's a common side dish. The potatoes are grated, shaped into circles, and fried in oil until crispy.

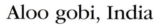

Perfect

Cottage pie, UK

Poor people who lived in small houses—called cottages—first ate this dish. It has a mashed potato topping and a ground-beef filling.

Aloo gobi, India

In North India, potatoes ("aloo") and cauliflower ("gobi") are often cooked together. This dish is sometimes called aloo gobi in restaurants.

Boiled new potatoes

Mehak, age 8, India

Llapingacho, Ecuador

This recipe originated in the Andes Mountains. The potatoes are mashed into a patty, filled with a soft cheese, and fried. The meal is usually served with peanut sauce and sausages.

POTATOES

Olivier salad, Russia

Let's celebrate! In Russia and its neighboring countries, children often eat potato salad at birthday parties.

Yaroslav, age 8, Russia

Jack, age 7, Ireland

Irish stew, Ireland

This one-pot dish contains potatoes, and lamb or mutton. It's a firm family favorite that has humble beginnings in rural Ireland.

Poutine, Canada

Poutine is a combination of fries, cheese curds, and gravy. It was voted one of the best Canadian inventions of all time!

Lauryn, age 8, Canada

Tortilla Española, Spain

Spanish omelets are made from potatoes and eggs. They are popular as a snack, as tapas (a light meal), and in packed school lunches.

Baked potatoes

Baked potatoes can be eaten as a side dish or as a main meal. In the UK, a baked potato is called a jacket potato, because of the crispy skin. Baked potatoes can be served with a variety of fillings. Here are four delicious options.

YOU WILL NEED:

• 4 baking or floury potatoes (e.g., Russets or Yukon Golds)

• 1 tbsp sunflower oil

• 1 tbsp coarse sea salt

Preheat the oven to 400°F (200°C). Prick each potato all over with a fork, then brush the skin with oil.

Put the salt on a shallow plate. Roll each potato in the salt and then place on a baking sheet.

Cook for 1 hour, or until the skin is crisp. Cut a cross in the top of each potato and squeeze apart. Top with your choice of filling.

Chili con carne

• 1 tsp sunflower oil

• 1 small onion, chopped

• 10oz (300g) lean ground beef or turkey

• 1–2 tsp chili powder, to taste

• 1 tsp ground cumin

• 14oz (400g) can chopped tomatoes

• 1 tbsp ketchup

• 14oz (400g) can red kidney beans, drained

1. Heat the oil in a frying pan and add the onion and ground beef. Cook over medium heat for 3–4 minutes, until browned. Stir in the spices, tomatoes, ketchup, and beans. **2.** Bring to a boil, then simmer for 10 minutes, until thickened. Spoon onto the potatoes.

Bacon and pineapple

- 8 strips of smoked bacon
- 2½oz (75g) cream cheese
- 4 pineapple rings, from a can, drained and chopped
- freshly ground black pepper

1. Dry-fry the bacon in a frying pan over medium heat for 2–3 minutes on each side, until crispy, then remove and drain on paper towels. **2.** Place the cheese in a small bowl and beat until softened, then stir in the pineapple and season. Break the bacon into small pieces. Spoon the pineapple mixture over the potatoes and sprinkle the crispy bacon over the top.

Baked beans and cheese

- 2 x 14oz (400g) cans baked beans
- 2½oz (75g) grated Cheddar cheese

Reheat the beans according to the instructions on the can, then spoon over the potatoes. Sprinkle the cheese on top.

In Brazil, a baked potato is called a *batata inglesa*, which means "English potato."

Tuna and corn

- 2 x 6oz (160g) cans tuna chunks, in water or brine, drained
- 4½oz (125g) corn from a can
- ¼ cup mayonnaise
- 2 scallions, chopped (optional)
- freshly ground black pepper

Place all the ingredients in a small bowl and combine. Season to taste. Spoon onto the potatoes.

Rafael, age 9, Brazil

Swedish hash

In Sweden, this dish is called *pyttipanna* meaning "teeny pieces in a pan." It's a great way of using up leftovers. The runny egg yolk makes a yummy topping.

TOP TIP
Fry the potatoes in a nonstick frying pan so the food doesn't stick to the pan.

YOU WILL NEED:

- 2 tbsp butter
- 2 tbsp sunflower oil
- 1lb 5oz (600g) potatoes, peeled and cut into ½in (1cm) cubes
- 2 onions, finely chopped
- 4 strips smoked bacon, chopped
- 14oz (400g) leftover roast meat (pork or beef), cut into ½in (1cm) cubes
- 2 hotdogs or smoked sausages, sliced
- 1 sprig fresh thyme, plus a few leaves for garnish
- Salt and freshly ground black pepper
- 4 eggs

Stella is from Sweden. This dish is popular in her country and in the countries nearby.

1 Heat the butter and 1 tbsp of the oil in a pan. When foaming, add the potatoes and onions. Fry for 15 minutes.

2 Cook the bacon in another pan over medium heat. When the fat starts to run, add the meat and sausages.

3 Add the fresh thyme. Fry the mixture over medium heat for 4–5 minutes, stirring occasionally.

4 Add the meat mixture to the potatoes and onions and mix thoroughly. Season to taste.

5 Heat the leftover oil in the pan you used to cook the meat. Crack open the eggs and add to the pan. Fry for 3–4 minutes.

6 Serve the hash on plates, with a fried egg on the top of each portion of hash. Sprinkle the remaining thyme on top.

Other STAPLES around the world

When the four main staples are in short supply, difficult to buy, or impossible to grow, people look to other food sources. These "other staples" range from milk and cheese to root vegetables and legumes.

Dairy products are cheese, butter, cream, and yogurt.

Dairy

The animals shown below provide milk for people to drink. Their milk is also used to make dairy products, which contain lots of protein and calcium.

Goats supply 2 percent of all milk. They are relied on in places where crops are hard to grow.

Goat

Cows produce 83 percent of the world's supply of milk.

Buffaloes make 13 percent of the milk that people drink around the world.

Cow

Buffalo

Sheep produce 1 percent of milk globally. They are relied on in areas that are arid.

Camels provide milk for people in dry areas. They account for half a percent of milk in the world.

Camel

Sheep

Bolat is from Kazakhstan, where cheese is made from horse milk.

Horse

The remaining 0.5% of milk comes from reindeer, yaks, horses, and donkeys.

Meat

Animal meat is eaten around the world because it's high in protein and provides lots of calories. Pork, poultry, and beef are eaten the most.

Poultry is the word used to describe meat derived from domestic birds, such as chickens, ducks, turkeys, and geese.

Chicken
Chicken meat is cheap to buy in most countries.

Turkey

Duck

Goose

Reindeer

Mattus is from Finland, where reindeer meat is popular.

Goat meat is lower in calories and fat than most other types of meat.

Lamb is the word for a baby sheep. It's eaten in lots of countries. Meat from an adult sheep is called mutton.

Sheep

Goat

People also eat meat from rabbits, deer, camels, and horses.

Pork is meat that comes from pigs. There are more than 180 species of pig.

Pig

Beef is meat that comes from cows. The average cow weighs 1,200lb (545kg).

Cow

Fish

Fish and seafood are also a common source of animal protein. More than one billion people around the world eat fish as their main protein.

Tuna

Popular fish are carp, catfish, cod, eel, haddock, halibut, herring, mackerel, salmon, sardine, scad, snapper, trout, and tuna.

Salmon

China is the world's biggest fishing nation. It catches and farms more fish than any other country.

Mackerel

Tai is from Vietnam. Fish and seafood are staples there.

Root vegetables

Grown under the soil, these hardy vegetables are packed with nutrients and filling carbohydrates.

Rafael lives in Brazil, where cassava is grown and eaten a lot.

Taro is a staple food in Fiji and other Pacific Island countries.

Taro

Cassava

Some people call sweet potatoes "yams," but they are two completely different root vegetables.

Yam

Sweet potato

Fruit

Although many fruits are sweet, sugary snacks, some are starchy or full of fat. These fruits are staples in the warm countries where they're grown.

Avocados were a staple in Central and South America for thousands of years.

Avocado

Breadfruit

Jackfruit

Jackfruits and breadfruits are grown for their nutritious skins. Jackfruits are huge—they grow up to 36in (90cm) long!

Olives were once a staple food in Greece, where Maria lives.

Olives

Plantain

Legumes

These foods are full of fiber and come from a family of plants called legumes. They grow on plants and are encased in pods.

Murk comes from Pakistan. Lentil dishes called "dal" are popular there.

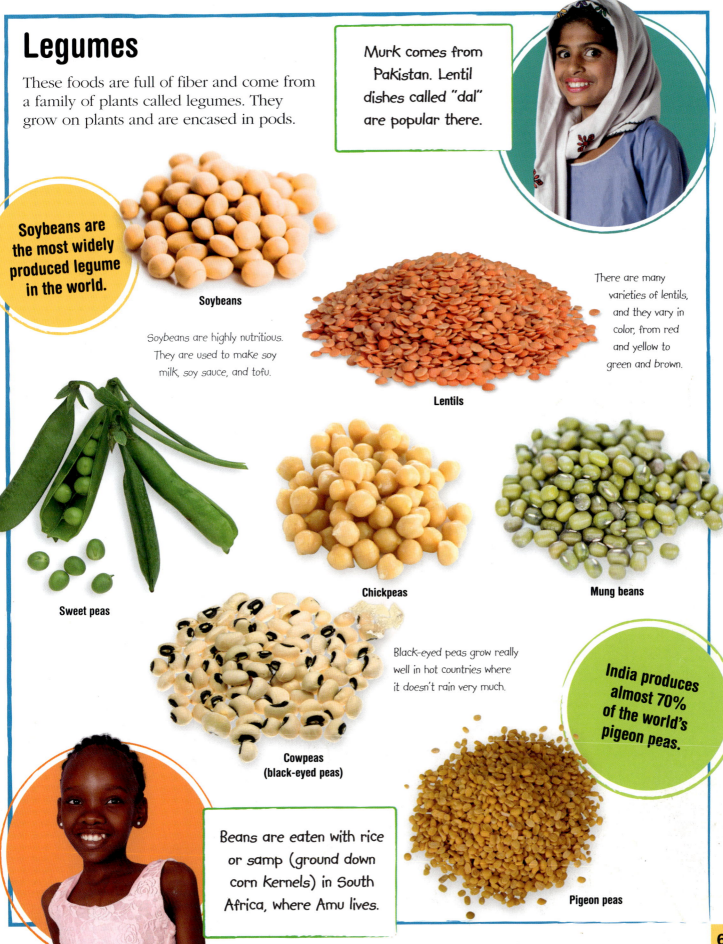

Soybeans are the most widely produced legume in the world.

Soybeans

Soybeans are highly nutritious. They are used to make soy milk, soy sauce, and tofu.

There are many varieties of lentils, and they vary in color, from red and yellow to green and brown.

Lentils

Sweet peas

Chickpeas

Mung beans

Black-eyed peas grow really well in hot countries where it doesn't rain very much.

India produces almost 70% of the world's pigeon peas.

Cowpeas (black-eyed peas)

Beans are eaten with rice or samp (ground down corn kernels) in South Africa, where Amu lives.

Pigeon peas

Milk

More than 80 percent of the world's **milk** supply comes from **cows**. Milk has more natural nutrients than any other drink. Cow's milk was first drunk by humans 10,000 years ago.

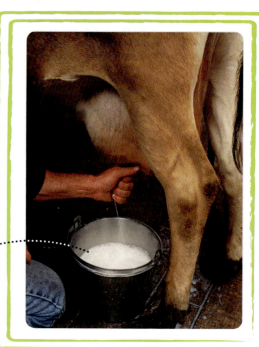

Milk is…

☑ full of calcium

☑ great for strong teeth and bones

Getting ready

Cow's milk is put through a process called pasteurization, which gets rid of any harmful germs.

Milking machines

A cow is ready to be milked when her udders are full. Milking used to be done by hand, but milking machines are far faster. One machine can milk 24 cows at a time.

There are 1.5 BILLION cows in the world.

A cow makes enough MILK each day to fill 144 GLASSES.

Milk is used in pancakes and crepes. Crepes are popular in France, where Morgan lives.

MILK PRODUCTS

About a quarter of all milk collected is used to make cheese. There are lots of different types of cheese. Milk is also used to make butter, yogurt, and ice cream.

Crepes

Recipes and methods for making crepes vary around the world. Try this sweet version.

YOU WILL NEED:

- 8in (20cm) nonstick frying pan
- ¾ cup all-purpose flour
- pinch of salt
- 2 eggs, beaten
- 1¼ cups milk
- 2 tbsp melted butter
- sunflower oil, for frying

TO SERVE:

- 1 banana, thinly sliced
- chocolate sauce

TOP TIP For a savory dish, fill the crepe with grated cheese and ham instead.

1 Sift the flour and salt into a large bowl. Gradually whisk in the eggs. Then slowly whisk in the milk, until the batter is smooth. Stir in the melted butter.

2 Heat a little of the oil in the pan. Add a large spoonful of batter and swirl it around to create a thin, even layer. Cook for 1–2 minutes, until golden.

3 Flip over and cook the other side for 1 minute. Remove from the pan. Make more crepes with the remaining batter, adding extra oil if needed.

Chicken

Long ago, people didn't know how to grow crops, so the first staple foods were **meat**. **Chicken** is one of the most widely eaten meats in the world.

EXCELLENT EGGS

Chickens are bred to produce good quality meat and eggs. Female chickens are kept on farms to lay eggs. Ancient Egyptians had chicken farms more than 4,000 years ago!

Chicken is...

☑ high in Vitamin B6 (good for the immune system)

☑ a good source of calcium

Farm facts

People used to raise chickens at home. Today, most chickens live on huge farms. Free-range chickens have room to move around outside.

Benefits

Chicken is a great source of nutrition. It's packed with protein, vitamins, and minerals, and is low in fat. Removing the skin before eating chicken reduces the fat content even more.

Egg cartons are cleverly shaped to keep eggs from cracking.

There are more than 19 BILLION chickens in the world.

In the UK, where Alec lives, people regularly eat roast chicken with vegetables and potatoes.

Chicken can be barbecued.

Roast chicken dinner

Kebabs

Try out these chicken kebabs or make a variety of your own using beef, lamb, or fish.

1

In a large bowl, mix the orange zest and juice, ginger, soy sauce, and honey. Season with pepper and mix well.

2

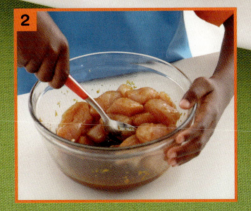

Add the chicken and stir to coat, then let marinate for 1–2 hours.

3

Thread the vegetables and chicken onto the skewers. Preheat the broiler and broil the kebabs for 12–15 minutes, turning once.

Sweet potatoes

Despite their name, **sweet potatoes** aren't potatoes, but one of the most widely eaten **root vegetables**. Often called a "superfood," they're a great source of energy and full of goodness.

Shoots are cut to become slips.

China produces most of the world's sweet potatoes.

SLIP GROWING

Most sweet potatoes are grown from "slips," which are the shoots that grow from a sweet potato. The shoots are cut off and left to grow roots, before being planted.

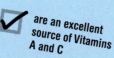

Sweet potatoes...

☑ are an excellent source of Vitamins A and C

☑ support your immune system

Sweet potatoes

Sweet potatoes can be mashed, boiled, roasted, or fried.

Lots of land

Sweet potato plants are traditionally grown in warm countries, but can now be grown in colder places, too. They take up a lot of space as they grow.

Colorful crop

Sweet potatoes can be orange, brown, red, or purple. Orange sweet potatoes have more beta-carotene than other varieties. Beta-carotene supports healthy skin.

Sweet potato wedges

Perfect as a side dish or snack, these wedges are a tasty treat and packed with lots of nutrients.

TOP TIP
This snack tastes great with dips, such as sour cream or ketchup.

1 Preheat the oven to 400°F (200°C). Cut each potato into 8 wedges, then place the wedges in a large bowl.

2 Pour the oil over the top, then add the garlic, herbs, and seasoning. Mix well with a spoon to coat all the wedges.

3 Place the wedges on a nonstick baking sheet in a single layer. Bake in the oven for 25–30 minutes (turning once), until golden and crispy.

YOU WILL NEED:

- 2 medium sweet potatoes, scrubbed
- 1 tbsp sunflower oil
- 2 cloves garlic, crushed
- 1 tsp dried thyme
- 1 tsp dried rosemary
- 1 tsp dried oregano
- salt and freshly ground black pepper

Plantains

Fruits that fill you up, such as avocados, breadfruit, and **plantains**, are a big part of people's diets. Plantains are closely related to bananas, but are more starchy and filling, and they have thicker skins.

UGANDA produces the most plantains in the world.

Growing plantains

Plantain plants aren't trees, but they can grow as tall as trees! Farmers like to grow them to medium height, because tall plants get damaged by wind.

Starchy staple

Plantains are a main source of carbohydrates for more than 70 million people. They are a staple food in African, Caribbean, and South and Central American countries.

Tostones

Ripe plantains are yellow with brown blotches.

Plantains start off green, then turn yellow, and finally black.

Black plantains are fine to eat, and very sweet inside.

TASTY TREATS

Green plantains are cooked in a similar way to potatoes. They are good for making plantain chips, such as the tostones, above.

Plantains are...

☑ high in fiber

☑ packed with potassium

☑ a good source of Vitamin C

Plantains are often grown and eaten in Colombia, where Miguel lives.

Plantain chips

These lightly spiced chips are baked, not fried. They taste great with a creamy dip.

TOP TIP
Allow the plantains to cool on the baking sheet for 5 minutes before serving.

YOU WILL NEED:

- 2 green plantains, peeled and cut into ¼in (5mm) slices
- 1 tbsp sunflower oil
- 1 tsp sea salt
- 1 tsp smoked paprika
- ½ tsp chili powder
- ½ tsp ground cumin

1 Preheat the oven to 400°F (200°C). Line 2 large baking sheets with parchment paper.

2 Put the plantains into a bowl and mix in the oil, salt, and spices, until evenly coated. Place the slices on the baking sheets.

3 Bake the slices for 15–20 minutes, until golden. Swap the baking sheets over halfway through and turn the chips.

Chickpeas

Legumes are a group of filling foods that includes peas, beans, and lentils. **Chickpeas**, also known as garbanzo beans, are one of the most widely grown legume crops.

Pod power

Chickpeas grow in pods on small, bushy plants. It takes about 100 days before they're ready to be picked. Chickpeas start off bright green and gradually become paler.

India GROWS, EATS, and IMPORTS the most chickpeas.

Old goodness

Chickpeas are high in nutrients. They were one of the first legumes to be grown by people. We've grown them for 7,500 years!

Chickpeas are...

☑ packed with manganese (good for healthy bones)

☑ full of fiber

There are 1–2 chickpeas per pod.

Chickpeas are a good meat substitute because they're full of protein.

Chickpeas can be ground into flour.

MAKING MEALS

Some people eat chickpeas just as they are, but others use them in popular dishes, such as falafel or hummus.

Hummus

Falafel

This Middle Eastern dish uses chickpeas as its main ingredient.

YOU WILL NEED:

- 2 x 14oz (400g) cans chickpeas, drained
- 2 garlic cloves, crushed
- 1 tbsp ground cumin
- 1 tsp ground coriander
- 1 tsp freshly ground black pepper
- 2 tbsp freshly chopped cilantro
- 1 large egg
- 2 tbsp toasted sesame seeds
- 1 tsp baking powder
- 1 tbsp oil, for frying

MINT DIP:
- ½ cup plain yogurt
- 2 tbsp freshly chopped mint
- ¼ cucumber, finely chopped

TOP TIP
Serve with toasted pita bread, chopped tomatoes, and the mint dip.

1 Pulse the chickpeas, garlic, spices, pepper, and fresh cilantro in a food processor until coarsely chopped. Add the egg, seeds, and baking powder. Pulse again.

2 Roll the mixture into 16 balls, then flatten slightly. Chill for 30 minutes. Preheat the oven to 375°F (190°C).

3 Fry the falafel in the oil over medium heat for 2–3 minutes on each side. Place on a baking sheet and bake for 10 minutes. Mix the dip in a bowl.

77

Equipment

It's important that you use the correct equipment for each task. Be careful with items that are sharp or require electricity to power them. Always have an adult present when you use them.

Spoons and spatulas

pasta spoon

wooden spatula

large plastic spoon

plastic spatula

wooden spoon

Kitchen basics

colander

set of plastic plates

oven mitts

plastic wrap

fork

table knife

dish towels

salt and pepper grinders

set of small glass bowls

set of plastic bowls

can opener

Frying, boiling, broiling, and stewing

broiler pan

frying pans

wok

saucepan with lid

grill pan

set of saucepans

Crushing, juicing, and blending

food processor

garlic press

handheld juicer

potato masher

Weighing and measuring

dry measuring cups

liquid measuring cup

scale

tablespoon

teaspoon

Baking

cookie cutters

large glass bowl

cooling rack

whisk

baking sheet

8in (20cm) square cake pan

pastry brush

sieves

rolling pin

icing piping bag

parchment paper

pizza pan

Cutting and chopping

scissors

pizza cutter

cutting boards

handheld grater

sharp knife

Extras

chopsticks

bamboo rolling mat

wooden skewers

INDEX

ACKNOWLEDGMENTS

DK would like to say a massive **thank you** to all the children who first appeared in *Children Just Like Me (CJLM)* and extend our thanks to the CJLM team. We'd also like to thank the children's photographers – Idris Ahmed, Andy Crawford, Vinh Dao Karin Duthie, Mulugeta Gebrekidan, Alan Keohane, Mike Merchant, and James Tye.

The *Food Like Mine* team would also like to thank James Mitchem, Sarah Foakes, and Magenta Fox for editorial assistance, Sakshi Saluja for picture credits, Rachael Hare for illustrations, and Anne Damerell for legal assistance. We'd also like to give a special thanks to our wonderful hand models: Anushka Campbell-Butler, NaZia Gifford, Jena Robb, Dylan Tannazi, and Skylar Thunberg.

The publisher would like to thank the following for their kind permission to reproduce their photographs:

(Key: a-above; b-below/bottom; c-center; f-far; l-left; r-right; t-top)

2-3 123RF.com: Oleg Doroshin (b). **3 123RF.com:** Feng Yu (ca); Natika (cl). **5 Dreamstime.com:** Eric Isselee (cla). **6 123RF.com:** Gilberto Mevi (c). **8 123RF.com:** Kitchakron sonnoy (clb); Photoroad (cra); Oleksii Olkin (crb). **Getty Images:** Andy Sacks (cla). **10-11 123RF.com:** Kitchakron sonnoy. **12 123RF.com:** Aliaksandr Mazurkevich (t). **13 123RF.com:** creativesunday (fcr); Thanyani Srisombut (tl); Nontawat Thongsibsong (tr); Varandah (cl); Kittiphat Inthonprasit (cr). **Getty Images:** Enrique Soriano / Bloomberg (clb). **14 123RF.com:** design56 (br); Jatesada Natayo (cra); Solomonjee (c); Junghwa You (c); Kevin Brine (bl). **15 123RF.com:** amylv (cr); Heinz tschanz-hofmann (tr); jirkaejc (ca); Fabrizio Troiani (bc). **16 123RF.com:** redhayabusa (cra). **iStockphoto.com:** pop_jop (tr, ca, c, crb). **17 Dreamstime.com:** Vtupinamba (br). **iStockphoto.com:** pop_jop (tc, tr, c, clb, cb). **24-25 Getty Images:** Andy Sacks. **26 123RF.com:** Katerina Skokanova (t). **27 123RF.com:** Natika (cb). **Alamy Stock Photo:** omphoto (crb). **iStockphoto.com:** Jovanjaric (crb). **28 123RF.com:** Francesco Dibartolo (cra). **29 123RF.com:** Martinak (cr). **30 123RF.com:** cokemomo (br).

iStockphoto.com: pop_jop (tc, ca, cb, crb). **31 123RF.com:** mors74 (c). **iStockphoto.com:** pop_jop (tl, ca, cr, cb). **40-41 123RF.com:** Photoroad. **42 123RF.com:** Shvadchak Vasyl (t). **43 123RF.com:** Steven Heap (cb). Dreamstime.com: Megalomaniac (cla). **44 123RF.com:** Arinahabich (cl); Hamsterman (bl). **45 123RF.com:** Bohuslav Jelen (c); yelo34 (tr); Kumruen Pakorn (cl); ildipapp (fclb); Yana Gayvoronskaya (clb); Sergey Skleznev (cb); Diana Taliun (bl); Svitlana Symonova (br). **Alamy Stock Photo:** Greg Wright (cr). **46 iStockphoto.com:** pop_jop (ca, cl, clb). **47 iStockphoto.com:** pop_jop (tr, ca, cr, cb, crb). **52-53 123RF.com:** Oleksii Olkin. **54 123RF.com:** Wilaiwan Jantra (t). **54-55 123RF.com:** Oleg Doroshin. **55 123RF.com:** Jakub Janele (clb); Pavel Rodimov (cla); lilkar (c); Leblond Catherine (cra). **57 123RF.com:** Denisfilm (bc); Feng Yu (clb). **Alamy Stock Photo:** Keith Leighton (c); Nacho Calonge (tr). **58 123RF.com:** Alexander Mychko (clb); Pablo Hidalgo (bc). **iStockphoto.com:** pop_jop (tr, ca, clb/Flag, cb). **58-59 123RF.com:** Yana Gayvoronskaya. **59 123RF.com:** vvoennyy (ftl). **iStockphoto.com:** pop_jop (tl, ca, cb, crb). **64 123RF.com:** Bennymarty (c); Eric Isselee (cr, br). **65 Dreamstime.com:** Eric Isselee (cr). **66 123RF.com:** Chatuphot Chatchawan (crb); Napat Polchoke (crb/Cut Jackfruit). **67 123RF.com:** Handmadepictures (cr); Joannawnuk (cla); Riccardo Motti (clb); PhotosIndia.com LLC (bc). **68** 123RF.com: Baloncici (c). **70 iStockphoto.com:** pop_jop

(cb). **72 123RF.com:** Suwit Gaewsee-ngam (cla). Dorling Kindersley: Moss Doerksen (cl). **74 123RF.com:** Chad Zuber (crb); Peter Zijlstra (cla); cokemomo (cb). **Alamy Stock Photo:** Pulsar Images (tr). **76 123RF.com:** Alexander Romanov (tl). Alamy Stock Photo: Danny Smythe (cb). **Cover images: Front:** 123RF.com: Inacio Pires br; **Getty Images:** Ken Davies b.

All other images © Dorling Kindersley

For further information see: www.dkimages.com

Andre, age 11, Australia

Meet children from around the world and find out about the foods that unite us all.